THE SECRETS OF TREES

GALLERY BOOKS

An Imprint of W. H. Smith Publishers Inc.
112 Madison Avenue
New York City 10016

This edition first published in U.S.
in 1991 by Gallery Books,
an imprint of W.H. Smith Publishers, Inc.
112 Madison Avenue, New York, New York 10016

ISBN 0-8317-9599-9

Printed and bound in Spain

For rights information about the photographs in
this book please contact:

The Image Bank
111 Fifth Avenue, New York, NY 10003

Producer: Solomon M. Skolnick
Writer: Ann Reilly
Design Concept: Lesley Ehlers
Designer: Ann-Louise Lipman
Editor: Joan E. Ratajack
Production: Valerie Zars
Photo Researcher: Edward Douglas
Assistant Photo Researcher: Robert V. Hale
Editorial Assistant: Carol Raguso

Title page: **The relatively short but massive trunk of the deciduous baobab tree *(Adansonia digitata)* is a familiar sight on the African savannah. Baobabs also grow wild in Australia, and are one of the largest, longest-lived, and economically useful trees in the world. *Opposite:* Autumn in the Rockies is heralded by the butter-yellow leaves of the quaking aspen *(Populus tremuloides)*, which contrast with the red leaves of another species.**

Perhaps the most famous lines written about trees were those penned by Joyce Kilmer in 1913:

> I think that I shall never see
> a poem lovely as a tree.

Lovely they are, but more than that, trees are living historical symbols with an economic and ecological importance unequaled by any other group of plants.

Trees are many things to different people, but by definition they are woody plants with a single trunk that grow at least 12 feet tall. Trees differ from shrubs in that shrubs are usually shorter, and have multiple stems springing directly from the ground. Although some jungle vines can grow several hundred feet into the canopy of a rain forest, their stems are weak and cannot support the plants. This characteristic distinguishes them from trees, which can, at least eventually, stand on their own.

Trees are classified into two categories: evergreen and deciduous. Those that paint the landscape in shades and tones of green all year are evergreens; those that shed their leaves are deciduous.

Evergreen trees are further divided into conifers and broad-leaved trees. Trees with needles, such as pines, firs, and spruces, and those with scalelike leaves, such as cedars and junipers, are called conifers, because they produce their seeds in cones. Almost all conifers are evergreen; the most notable exception to this are the larches (genus *Larix*), the dawn redwood (*Metasequoia glyptostroboides*), and the bald cypress (*Taxodium distichum*), which shed their needles in fall.

Although the quaking aspen is thought of as being synonymous with the Rocky Mountains, it actually has the widest range of any tree in North America. The quaking aspen is found from Newfoundland south to Delaware and west in a broad belt to Alaska.

Preceding page: The quaking aspen was so named for the continual movement of its leaves. According to Christian legend, Judas hanged himself on this tree and its leaves have trembled in shame ever since. Actually, the tree and its quaking leaves were growing at least 70 million years before Christ. *This page, above:* Aspen wood, relatively worthless as firewood, has been used for corral fences, horse stalls, tongue depressors, popsicle sticks, high-quality paper, and, when shredded, as a packing material for upholstered furniture and as protection for perishable vegetables. *Right:* The flowers of Indian paintbrush pop up through a carpet of ponderosa pine *(Pinus ponderosa)* cones. Once a pine cone is pollinated, its scales close up tight and remain so for two years until the cone matures and dries. Then, the hard, woody scales open to release the seeds.

The needles of pine trees grow in bundles of two, three, or five: Those with bundles of two or three needles are known as "hard" pines. *Below:* Pines are producers of resins including pitch, used since at least biblical times to waterproof boats; and rosin, which is rubbed on such diverse articles as violin bows and ballet shoes to prevent slippage. *Opposite:* The ponderosa pine is the second tallest pine; it averages 80 to 150 feet in height but can reach a towering 200 feet. Only the sugar pine *(Pinus lambertiana)* grows taller.

All deciduous trees are broad leaved, as are a small number of evergreens such as the rhododendron *(Rhododendron arboreum)*, live oak *(Quercus virginiana)*, and southern magnolia *(Magnolia grandiflora)*.

Of the 60,000 to 70,000 species of trees in the world that have already been identified by botanists, a few hundred are palms, about 500 are conifers, and the rest are broad-leaved trees. About 865 different species of trees from 222 genera are native to or naturalized in the continental U.S. The most notable of these are in the pine, yew, palm, maple, cashew, walnut, beech, birch, magnolia, laurel, rose, and willow families. Tree species comprise about three and one-half percent of the plant species in the U.S. They are certainly far from the largest group of plants, but they set records in many other ways.

Trees have been in existence since the Devonian period of the Paleozoic era, which dates back about 400 million years, hundreds of millions of years before humans were here to enjoy them. The maidenhair tree *(Gingko biloba)* is the oldest known surviving tree. Fossil records of the genus date back 200 million years. In fact, the fossils were known before the trees, and the tree was thought to be extinct until it was found growing in a temple garden in Japan. The gingko is a plant rarity, as it is the only deciduous, coniferous tree with broad leaves.

Left: A harsh and uninviting environment is home to this battered, windswept specimen growing at Olmsted Point in Yosemite National Park in California. *Below:* A middle-aged ponderosa pine stands alone next to the sandstone striations on Checkerboard Mesa in Utah's Zion National Park. When ponderosa pines pass the century mark, the bark turns yellow-brown, giving them their second common name, western yellow pine. *Overleaf:* A Montana forest, composed mainly of deciduous, coniferous larches, glistens in the winter sun.

The conifer and cycad families predate gingkos, but none of the original cycads or conifers are still in existence today. Flowering trees date to the Jurassic period of the Mesozoic era, about 160 million years ago, and by about the time that people first walked on earth, virtually every tree genus now in existence was growing profusely.

About 300 million years ago, there were huge forests of trees unlike most of the trees that grow today. Many of these were club mosses and horsetail trees. They still exist, but only as small perennial plants, not trees. Over time, the trees died, became buried, and turned into coal. In other places, buried forests became *petrified*, or turned into stone. One of the best places to view this phenomenon is at the Petrified Forest National Park in Arizona, where fossils of trees that died 100 million years ago can be seen.

The normal age span of trees is different for each species. Some birches live only about 40 years, whereas the sugar maple (*Acer saccharum*) can live for 500 years. Although the gingko is the oldest living species, the oldest living individual trees are the bristlecone pines (*Pinus aristata*), which grow

This page, top to bottom: The tamarack, eastern, or American larch *(Larix laricina)* is one of the hardiest trees, surviving winters as cold as -50° Fahrenheit. The western larch *(Larix occidentalis)* is the only commercially important larch native to North America and yields strong and durable timber; its cousin, the European larch *(Larix decidua)* is the source of valuable Venetian turpentine as well as lumber. Pacific Northwest ice frosts a western red cedar *(Thuja plicata)*, whose soft yet durable wood is used for shingles and siding. *Opposite:* Members of the genus *Thuja* are sometimes known as *arborvitae*, or "tree of life," because they can live for several hundred years. In the wild, they provide deer with food and shelter; they are also a common garden ornamental because of their slow, compact growth.

Preceding page: Western red cedar is also known as giant arborvitae, because it can reach heights of 200 feet, as well as great ages, in its natural habitat from Alaska south into California. *This page:* The Sitka spruce *(Picea sitchensis)* is the biggest and fastest-growing spruce in the world. Along the coastline of Washington state, trees can grow 200 feet high and 50 feet or more around at the base.

When David Douglas discovered the Douglas fir in 1825, he thought it was a pine, but later botanists decided to create a new genus and species to fit the tree—*Pseudotsuga menziesii*. *Below:* Today, 25 percent of all the timber cut in the U.S. is Douglas fir (left), replacing the Eastern white pine *(Pinus strobus)*, as the country's dominant timber tree. Massive trunks of Sitka spruce (right), a tree also discovered by David Douglas, are topped with the prickliest needles of any American spruce. *Opposite:* The Douglas fir is one of the tallest trees in the world, averaging 250 feet in height. Its massive trunks were once used as masts on wooden sailing vessels.

The stately trunks of lodgepole pines *(Pinus contorta* var. *latifolia)* are reflected in the tranquil waters of Lake Louise in Banff National Park, Alberta, Canada. *Below:* Lodgepole pines have straight trunks and lightly furrowed bark. In contrast, their close relatives, shore or beach pines *(Pinus contorta)*, are shorter, scrubby plants with deeply furrowed bark and much stronger wood. *Opposite:* The bristlecone pine *(Pinus aristata)* is the oldest living thing on earth: A record-setting tree in the Inyo National Forest's Schulman Grove is believed to be at least 4,600 years old.

on rocky mountainsides and are one of the first trees to grow below the timberline. Even when they are dead, their contoured branches and swirling grains make these trees things of beauty. The oldest, growing in California's White Mountains in the Inyo National Forest, is believed to be more than 4,600 years old, making it the oldest living thing on earth. The largest bristlecone pine is believed to be 1,500 years old.

Although some giant sequoias *(Sequoiadendron giganteum)* are over 3,000 years old, even these are not as old as bristlecone pines. But no trees are more massive than giant sequoias, some of which measure more than 100 feet around at the base. The largest giant sequoia, the General Sherman Tree in Sequoia National Park in California, was 275 feet tall and had a circumference of 82 feet in 1975, when it was last measured.

Like giant sequoias, redwoods *(Sequoia sempervirens)* are relics of the ancient past, some believed to be 3,500 years old, and are the world's tallest plants, reaching heights of over 300 feet. The largest coast redwood in the world, at Humboldt Redwoods National Park in California, was 362 feet tall when it was last measured in 1972.

Dwarfing the observer, the giant sequoia trees *(Sequoiadendron giganteum)* of California are the most massive on earth, measuring over 100 feet around at the base. *Opposite:* Giant sequoias grow only on the western slopes of the Sierra Nevada at elevations of close to a mile or more, in groves that total 35,000 acres. *Following page:* It is estimated that the largest giant sequoia, known as the General Sherman Tree, weighs 12 million pounds and would yield more than 600,000 board feet of lumber if felled.

Other trees that have broken height records are a Port Orford cedar (*Chamaecyparis lawsoniana*) in Siskiyou Forest in Oregon that measures 219 feet; a coast Douglas fir (*Pinus strobus*) in Olympic National Park in Washington that rises to 221 feet; a ponderosa pine (*Pinus ponderosa*) in Plumas, California that stands 223 feet high; and a noble fir (*Abies nobilis*) in Gifford Pinchot National Forest in Washington that is 278 feet tall. Many of Australia's various eucalyptus trees measure over 300 feet in height. The thickest tree trunk is that of a Mexican bald cypress (*Taxodium mucronatum*) in Oaxaca, Mexico. It measures over 40 feet in diameter, or over 125 feet around the base.

Broad-leaved tree species outnumber the coniferous tree species in the U.S. by at least six to one. Worldwide, there are nearly 500 species of conifers in seven families, most of which are native to the Northern Hemisphere. The pine family, which includes pine, spruce, fir, and hemlock, is the largest and best known. Members of the pine family are prized for lumber as well as other products such as turpentine and resins. Two coniferous families are found primarily south of the equator, and

Preceding page: Coast redwoods (*Sequoia sempervirens*) are the tallest trees in the world; the largest, located in Redwoods National Park in California, measures over 360 feet in height. *This page, top to bottom:* Redwoods and their relatives have been on earth for about 125 million years. Largely protected today, redwoods once were heavily lumbered; over one-third of California's original 2 million acres of redwood forest were cut down between 1850 and 1925. The hemispherical growth on this redwood tree is a source of burl, a hard wood used in making veneers and inlays for furniture. *Opposite:* John Muir, who founded the Sierra Club in 1892, is the person most associated with redwoods. He was the force behind Sequoia National Park, and in 1907, Muir Woods National Monument was established in his honor.

Preceding page: Club Moss Trail in Olympic National Forest in Washington is home to plants that dominated forests about 300 million years ago. Today club mosses exist as low-growing perennials, although they were once trees. *This page, right:* Collectively, conifers account for 75 percent of the world's timber and almost all of the pulp for its paper. *Below:* Mosses and ferns drape tree branches in the Hoh Rain Forest in Olympic National Park, Washington.

include a strange-looking tree with
snakelike branches and sharp, scaly
leaves, called the monkey puzzle
tree (*Araucaria araucana*).

Of all the broad-leaved trees
in North America, the mighty oak
trees are the most widespread,
occupying the greatest variety of
habitats and comprising the largest
number of species, perhaps as many
as 75. Oaks are members of the
beech family and are also related
to chestnuts. Venerated and even
worshiped in ancient times, oaks
provide the most important hard-
wood timber for lumber, fuel
barrels, and railroad ties, among
other things. In years when the
acorn crop fails, deer, squirrels,
and raccoons may have trouble
finding enough to eat.

Maples, next to oaks, are the
best-known broad-leaved trees.
There are at least 80 species known
worldwide, about 25 percent of them
from North America. Pollution-
resistant Norway maples (*Acer
platanoides*) shade city streets;
Japanese species lend decoration to
many gardens. Although all maples
produce a sweet sap in late winter
and early spring, only the sugar
maple (*Acer saccharum*) contains
enough sugar to warrant tapping
and boiling for syrup and candy.

The growth of the trunks of
oaks, maples, and most other trees
is always lateral, never vertical. It
is the branches that give vertical
growth. This is why a nail ham-
mered into a tree trunk never
reaches a different height than that
at which it was originally placed. As
the tree trunk grows laterally, it
forms one growth ring each year.
These can be counted, when a tree
is cut down, to find the accurate age
of the tree.

**Autumn colors the slopes of the Great
Smoky Mountains, whose deciduous
forests extend from Tennessee into
North Carolina.**

The most distinctive American hickory (left) is the shagbark hickory *(Carya ovata)*. Hickory, along with black locust and live oak, is one of the best woods to burn in a fireplace, because it generates a lot of heat, is slow burning, and is low in smoke production. The American sycamore *(Platanus occidentalis)* (right) is the largest in bulk of any North American deciduous tree. It is readily identified by its peeling bark, its round seed balls, and its large, single-bladed leaves. *Below:* White ash *(Fraxinus americana)* is the wood of choice for baseball bats, wooden tennis rackets, and hockey sticks because of its strength, elasticity, and shock resistance.

A leafless American elm *(Ulmus americana)* is silhouetted against the twilight sky. The elm was a common tree of village squares before Dutch elm disease reached U.S. shores in 1930 and destroyed an estimated 100 million trees. *Below:* Elm wood has an interlocking, shock-resistant grain that makes it perfect for chair seats. Water resistant as well, it has been used in ship keels, pier pilings, buckets, and pipes.

As spring arrives in Vermont, sugar maple *(Acer saccharum)* trees are tapped for their sap, 30 to 40 gallons of which produce one gallon of maple syrup. Although Vermont leads the U.S. in maple syrup production, Quebec, Canada produces 75 percent of the world's supply. *Below:* Three states — Vermont, Wisconsin, and New York, have chosen the sugar maple as their state tree, and Rhode Island has chosen an unspecified maple. Colored red, the maple leaf is the symbol of Canada.

The reds, oranges, and golds of the maple have brought tourists scurrying to New England in the fall to view the colorful spectacle. *Below:* Maples are known for their strength, and were therefore used in ancient times for spears and in modern times for furniture and cabinetry.

Rings tell more than age, though. Those closest to the outside of the trunk are close together, indicating that a tree's growth slows as it matures. Those in the center, which are the widest apart, indicate the rapid growth of the tree when it was young. In older trees, wide distances between some rings show that the tree grew rapidly that year, indicating good weather. Small distances between other rings show that the tree grew slowly, suggesting drought conditions or shading by nearby larger trees. Scars can indicate occurrences of forest fires. Much has been learned about weather and growing conditions in the past by studying the rings of very old trees.

The trunk of the tree supports and sustains leaves, flowers, and fruit. The trunk is composed of five sections, each one adapted to a different function. The outside is the *bark*, which protects the tree from changes in temperature and humidity. The *liber*, or *bast*, is beneath the bark, and is the tissue through which sap descends. This is the part of the trunk that forms rings. The *cambium* is the next layer, which is responsible for the

Preceding page: The toothed, usually three-lobed leaf of the maple is easy to identify, and here contrasts in an autumn scene with the golden-leaved, white-barked birch. Most U.S. maples are found east of the Mississippi River. *This page, top to bottom:* White birch *(Betula papyrifera)* is also known as paper birch or canoe birch; it has been used over the years for canoes, baskets, roof shingles, clothing, paper, food, thread spools, clothespins, and toothpicks. Many birches are pioneer trees, growing rapidly on bare soil, offering shade to the next group of plants that encroach, and dying at an early age, usually 40 to 60 years old. The amazingly flexible birch, which can right itself after being bent over with heavy snow, has been used in brooms and as a "switch" by old-fashioned schoolmasters to keep their wards in line.

Oaks are the most common trees in North America, comprising as many as 75 of the 450 species known worldwide. An average oak tree may take as many as 100 years to mature and may live for as many as 450 years. *Left:* Most oaks start to bear acorns when they are about 10 years old, and can produce 5,000 acorns each year. *Opposite:* The strong wood of the mighty oak, which originated in Asia about 90 million years ago, has been used for furniture and ship keels for centuries. One species of oak is the source of cork. *Overleaf:* Forests provide us with oxygen, newspapers, lumber, and one-third of our fuel, among other things. In the U.S., 34 percent of the land is forested, compared to 51 percent in the Soviet Union, and none in Egypt.

Pine needles are resistant to weather extremes and most insects. Although pines are evergreens, the needles do not last forever; depending on the species, they live anywhere from two to 30 years before they fall off and are replaced. *Below:* The several different species of southern yellow pine (left) are hard pines, since their wood is not as easy to work as that of the soft pines. They are, however, a major source of pitch. The new spring growth of a pine tree (right) is called a candle, a word that describes the growth's shape until it fully opens. The immature female cones will eventually be pollinated by some of the 1 to 2 million pollen grains produced by every male pine cone each year.

growth of the tree. Next is the *wood* itself, which transports sap up to the leaves. Finally the *pith*, or *medulla*, is the core of the tree from which the other parts grow. In some trees, this part disappears when the tree reaches a certain age, leaving a hollow center.

All rules have exceptions, and palm trees are the exception to lateral growth. Of the roughly 2,500 different kinds of palms, most have no branches. The trunk of a young palm first grows thick and produces more and larger leaves each year. When the trunk reaches adult thickness, the tree then begins to grow taller, but the trunk never gets any thicker. Because their manner of growth is different from other trees, palm trees do not have rings.

The "knees" of the bald cypress rise from the roots to above the water line. Scientists believe the knees may provide oxygen for the roots, additional support for the tree, or both. *Below:* The bald cypress *(Taxodium distichum)* is a towering tree of southern swamps whose flaring or buttressed trunk rises out of mud covered by shallow water.

More closely related to grasses and bamboo than they are to oaks and maples, palms are important trees of the tropics and the source of coconuts, dates, and hearts-of-palm. The largest seeds in the world are the nuts of the double coconut palm (*Lodoicea maldivica*) of the Seychelles, which may weigh 50 pounds each.

Cycads look like palm trees, with a branchless trunk and a crown of long, feathery leaves. However, they are more closely related to pines, since they produce seeds in large cones. Millions of years ago, cycads grew in almost every part of the world, but now they grow only in the tropical areas of Africa, Asia, and Central America.

In some parts of the world, trees grow in thick forests. In other places, they do not grow at all. To grow, a tree needs a period of more than two months each year without frost, certain soil conditions deter-mined by the needs of the particular species, and adequate water and light. The few trees that grow in the Arctic never reach full size, and no trees can survive the bitter ice and cold of Antarctica. Few trees grow in the desert, except in oases, because there is not usually enough water.

One of the most appealing aspects of deciduous trees is their signaling of autumn by the chang-ing color of their leaves. Leaves are green because they contain

The bald cypress is one of the rare conifers, along with dawn redwood and larch, that loses its needles over the winter. Its wood is light but durable and is used for vats, shingles, and railroad ties.

chlorophyll, the substance plants use to make food for themselves. Other pigments, including red, yellow, and orange, are present in leaves, but are masked by the green. But as the days shorten in fall, chlorophyll production stops and the green color disappears. The brilliant colors of fall dominate until the leaves fall from the trees.

The leaves of all green plants and particularly those of trees, since they are so numerous, are fundamental to life. Chlorophyll enables green plants to produce food directly from light. This process is known as *photosynthesis.* It is the basis of the lives not only of the plants, but of all creatures who feed on the leaves, or who feed on animals who eat the leaves – it is the basis of all life on earth.

During the process of photosynthesis, oxygen is released from the plant, and carbon dioxide is consumed. Without this exchange, the atmosphere which surrounds earth would be unsuitable for any form of life.

But other parts of trees also provide food for animals and people. Most nuts, such as walnuts, pecans, chestnuts, pistachios, and almonds are actually seeds that

This page, top to bottom: **Black mangroves** *(Avicennia germinans),* **such as this one at Everglades National Park in Florida, help to build up and retain soil along subtropical and tropical coves, rivers, swamps, and lagoons. In addition to binding and building the soil, the sturdy, arching prop roots of the red mangrove** *(Rhizophora mangle)* **serve as a nursery for mollusks, crustaceans, young fish, and algae. Bromeliads, such as these of the genus** *Guzmania,* **are epiphytes that use trees for support but obtain their food and water from rain and air.** *Opposite:* **This lone Monterey cypress** *(Cupressus macrocarpa),* **a famous landmark along 17 Mile Drive near Carmel, California, has scaly leaves that are coated with wax, making the tree resistant to fire, dry soil, and saltwater spray.**

The coconut palm *(Cocos nucifera)* is found in tropical settings all over the world. It provides us, in addition to coconuts, with coconut oil, coconut milk, hearts of palm, fiber (from the husks), and sugar and alcohol (from the flowers.) *Below:* Palms (left) are actually more closely related to grasses than they are to other trees. As with grasses, their leaf veins are parallel and their seedlings have only one leaf, not two. Palm leaves (right), known as fronds, are used to thatch roofs and to make mats, baskets, hats, and decorations. *Opposite:* There are over 200 different genera and almost 3,000 different species of palms, the most well known of which are the coconut and date palms.

Preceding page: Many vines, like the lianas growing in the Amazon basin, are woody, but unlike trees, they do not grow a trunk and rely on other plants for upright support. *This page, right:* The kauri pine *(Agathis australis)* is one of the most outstanding trees for size, beauty, and timber value, and is the source of resinous copal. Here it supports a number of epiphytes. *Below:* Prop roots, buttressing the base of the tree to give it support, are common sights in tropical rain forests such as this one in Costa Rica.

grow on trees. Apples, pears, peaches, oranges, persimmons, pomegranates, cherries, and in fact, most fruits, are borne on trees.

Besides fruits and nuts, many other edible and potable products come from trees. Gin, for example, is flavored with the berries of the common juniper (*Juniperus communis*); chewing gum is made from the tropical sapodilla tree (*Achras zapota*). Coffee, chocolate, cloves, and nutmeg all come from tropical trees.

Trees are the source, too, of all kinds of materials used in manufacturing. Lumber to build houses, mahogany and teak for fine furniture, and paper for magazines, books, and newspapers all come from trees. Prehistoric people knew the value of trees, and used their wood to make spears, boats, and the first wheel. Native Americans used the bark of the paper birch (*Betula papyrifera*) to make canoes, baskets, dishes, and trays. Long before the advent of plastics and even before the Bronze or Iron ages, wood was used to make tools, handles, and containers.

This page, top to bottom: **Once the banana plant (*Musa* spp.) has flowered and fruited, it dies, but a new plant will spring up at its base. In addition to being a source of food (there are over 300 different edible forms of bananas), banana trees are used for roofs, cattle feed, clothing, medicine, dye, alcohol, wine, vinegar, and packing material. Many of the plants grown in homes and offices across North America, such as ferns and wandering Jew, are common sights under the canopy of a tropical jungle.** *Opposite:* **The banyan tree (*Ficus benghalensis*) is a close relative of the fig. Its aerial roots grow earthward from horizontal branches to support the huge evergreen tree, one of which in India measured 2,000 feet across.**

Since the earliest days of humanity, wood has been used for fuel. Currently, about half the trees harvested worldwide are used as fuel. Some are burned in individual homes, but the vast majority of this wood feeds generators that produce electricity. Similarly, more than 3 billion metric tons of coal, formed by ancient trees, are mined throughout the world each year. 60 percent of the coal sold in the U.S. is purchased by plants that generate electricity.

The bark of trees also provides a wealth of useful products. The bark of oaks and some other trees contains tannic acid, essential to the tanning industry in converting animal hides into leather. The spongy bark of a type of oak that grows in the Mediterranean region provides cork. The bark of the *Cinchona calisaya* tree contains quinine, used by doctors to treat malaria and other diseases; quinidine, which also comes from this bark, is used to treat some types of heart disease. Cinnamon comes from the bark of *Cinnamomum zeylanicum*, which is removed and dried.

The psychological benefits humans receive from trees are untold. In spring, the soft green of new leaves lightens winter-weary hearts. In autumn the brilliant hues of red, orange, yellow, and gold quickens pulses. The winter holidays would not be the same without Christmas trees, boughs of holly with shiny leaves and red berries, and wreaths made from sweetgum balls. In large, industrial cities, where the downtowns are grim, life would be even more depressing if trees did not add to the quality of life.

Bamboo trees are actually giant grasses, growing primarily in the tropical areas of the world. They are used as ornamentals, for erosion control, for furniture, and as water pipes.

The flat-topped acacia tree is a common sight on the East African plains of Kenya and Tanzania. These trees grow very quickly, but are not long lived. *Left:* The acacia is the favorite diet of giraffes, which are tall enough to reach its branches. Acacias are covered with thorns and stinging ants, which do not bother the giraffes, but keep other animals away. *Opposite:* The trunk of the baobab tree *(Adansonia digitata)* is often hollow and can hold up to 250 gallons of water. The leaves, bark, and fruits are used for food, rope, paper, thread, medicine, and clothing.

There are over 500 species and 100 named varieties of eucalyptus. They are native to Australia and Tasmania, but have been introduced into the warmer areas of North America. In California, they are a common street tree. *Below:* Eucalyptus trees (left) are known by a variety of common names, which indicate the type of bark they have. Those known as "gums" have smooth bark that flakes off every year. Other eucalyptus trees (right) are called "ironbark" because the bark is hard, fissured, and dark colored; yet others are called "stringybark" because the bark is long and fibrous. *Opposite:* Eucalyptus trees are a source of timber, gum, tannin oil, eucalyptus oil, and decorative leaves which can be dried and used in flower arrangements. They are the most important forest tree in Australia.

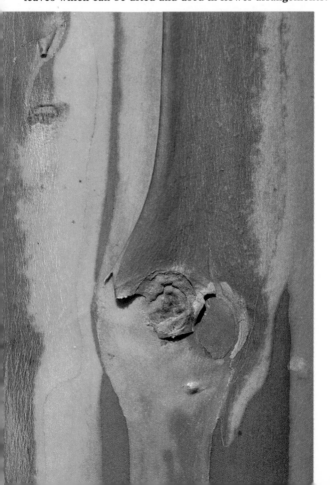

Childhood memories are often filled with visions of trees – a favorite felled by a storm, or a newly planted sapling reaching toward the sky. Perhaps a long, summer-day picnic under the shady branches of an elm or an afternoon spent lolling in a hammock strung between two pines comes to mind. Adolescents carve their initials and those of their true loves into a tree's bark; adults remember departed loved ones by planting trees in their memories.

We have much to thank trees for, because not only do they make life on earth possible, they also make it tastier, healthier, more beautiful, and more enjoyable.

This page, top to bottom: Native to southern Peru and Bolivia, the stiff, giant bromeliad *Puya raimondii* has clumps of leaves that can be eight feet across and a flower spike that can grow to 25 feet or more. The grass tree (*Xanthorrhoea* spp.), an Australian perennial with a palmlike trunk and grasslike leaves, produces a substance known as acaroid resin (which is used in varnishes) at the base of old leaves of some species. The Joshua tree *(Yucca brevifolia)* can grow 40 feet high and has been honored with its own national monument in California. *Opposite:* The thickened stems of cactus plants store water and carry on photosynthesis, since most cactus plants do not have leaves. Spines, which are found on most cacti, protect the plant from animal attackers.

Native to the southwestern U.S. and northern Mexico, the elephant tree *(Bursera microphylla)* grows four to 10 feet tall and has branches that explain its common name. *Left:* As an elephant tree matures, the outer bark peels off and reveals a new bark. Elephant trees are aromatic and have a resinous sap. *Opposite:* The bizarre boojum tree *(Idria columnaris)* has a soft, often hollow trunk that can grow 50 feet high and is covered with small leaves and large spines. Its yellow flower panicles may be as long as 16 inches.

INDEX OF PHOTOGRAPHY

TIB indicates The Image Bank